Tweedy
The Little Amp Who Found His Song

Story and Photos by Gary Benson

NEWMAN SPRINGS PUBLISHING
320 Broad Street
Red Bank, NJ 07701

First originally published by Newman Springs Publishing 2021

ISBN 978-1-64801-163-4 (Paperback)
ISBN 978-1-64801-164-1 (Digital)

Printed in the United States of America

Dedicated to
my encouraging family, friends
and to Leo Fender, the inventor of this wonderful
little 1954 Fender 4-watt amp.

A long, long time ago, there was a little Fender amp, born in Fullerton,

California. His name was 'Champ' Tweed 5C-1 — small, insignificant — designed for a beginning electric guitar player and nothing more.

The "coat" he wore was Tweed — popular to wear in his day, as many of his luggage and guitar case friends were covered that way. Yet, in spite of this classy covering, his older brothers and cousins, Twin Tweed and Princeton, teased him incessantly because of his small size, low wattage, and insignificance to do anything important in the music world.

Tweedy did know that some of his little amp friends had gone on to recording studios to be part of some very famous songs because of their small size like him, *but a future like that seemed very far away right now.*

As the years passed, Tweedy muddled through life in obscurity.

At some point, someone set their cigarette upon his cabinet, forever leaving scars in remembrance of some far gone party night performance.

Tweedy eventually ended up in a thrift store, his voice silenced by neglect and void of tone, not producing any sounds at all.

Then one day, a customer spotted Tweedy and saw something with promise.

He picked Tweedy up for a song, $20, and took him to the amp repairman where Tweedy was brought back to life. The amp repair guy said,

"Well, they are unique, but no one takes them very seriously."

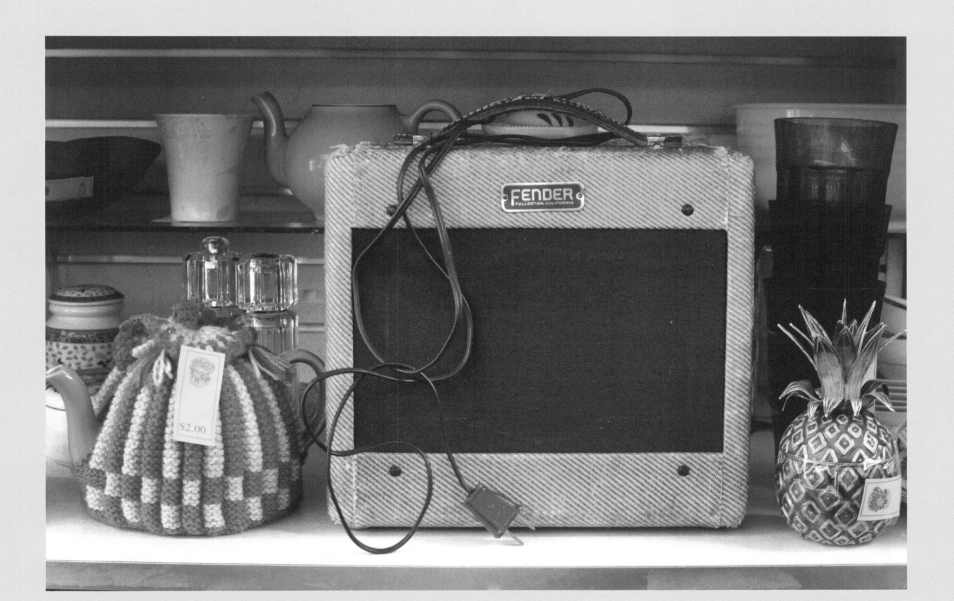

And so Tweedy excitedly went home with his new owner, hoping for a new life together.

That hope was there, but did not materialize. Tweedy's new owner lost interest in his small volume of sound and resigned to putting Tweedy in the closet as a passing interest.

Tweedy sat amongst the clothes, shoes, and t-shirts that surrounded him in disarray and neglect. At night, he cried silent tears as the closet doors were shut to keep the cat out.

After about a year of being forgotten, lonely and never plugged in, Tweedy was put up for sale again. The days went by, and Tweedy's frustrated owner lowered the price.

Tweedy felt very low at this time, feeling he was not important to anybody.

Then one day, someone came to try Tweedy out. He was intrigued by it's history and legacy of being an early electric guitar amp and the model that many famous rock songs were recorded on.

But when he showed up to see Tweedy, he was taken aback . . .

. . . *"I had no idea it was so small".*

And it was not loud like other amps he had as he gave it a test play.

Then the prospective buyer thought about Tweedy for a minute. "When will I see something like this again?"

So he took a gamble and said, "I'll buy it."

And Tweedy was loaded into his car and taken to a new home, not certain what his future would be.

The new owner tried Tweedy on different guitars; some sounded good, others did not. He was not sure what to make of this tiny amp. "Did I make a mistake buying this?" he thought with a twinge of regret. Tweedy's feelings again took another hit. But as the owner thought about it, he said, *"It does have a classic sound."*

So little Tweedy sat amongst his new owner's larger and louder amps, wondering if anybody would ever find him important again.

Yet, in his new owner's mind, something was special about this little amplifier from an important era in electric guitar history; he just was not sure what "it" was.

Two long years passed; again, Tweedy felt forgotten, sad, and lonely.

Then one day, the owner reached a "stretching" decision — he was going to play his electric guitar in the church worship band — a first for him.

Primarily an acoustic player, he had some electric guitars but told his friends, "Well, I play electric, but only in the basement by myself where no

one can hear me." Now he was taking a chance to learn something new in his musical journey; but what amp would be the right one to use?

He tried Tweedy's relative, Pro Junior with the band. His cousin had more wattage, but the sound guy at the church said, "Let's keep the volume down, put it behind the stage wall out of sight, mic it, and run it through the sound board. With that technique, I can control the sound better in the room."

Tweedy's owner was skeptical, but thought he'd give it a try. The results were amazing; a good mic on this amp did wonders! Then the sound guy asked, "Do you have anything smaller in wattage?" Tweedy"s owner said, "Yes, I do…but really? Smaller in wattage than what we are using?" He replied, "Yes, bring it next time, and I'll show you."

He told him about the 4 -watt Tweedy 5C-1 from 1954, and he said,

"For sure, let's try it!"

So he brought Tweedy in, who was about twice the size of a kid's lunch box to the church and plugged him in behind the stage; he put a mic on the cabinet, turned the volume up to the mid-position, and flicked the switch on to see the little red 'jewel' power light glow.

Tweedy thought, "What just happened to me? . . . I'm back to life again!"

This is my big chance to shine . . . but can I . . . can I . . . will I? Tweedy thought, "Here I am, behind this wall, where nobody can see me. Oh, how I want to be on the stage showing what I can do and have people love me. Why am I back here behind everything?"

Just then, practice got called short, and Tweedy was turned off; he never had a chance for anyone to hear him. Would he ever get another chance?

That night, Tweedy had a dream; a dream of being on the stage in the sanctuary, prominent in his place, his owner looking back at him waiting for the hall to fill with people to hear him and his sound.

His slumber broke as he awoke, facing the reality of being stuck behind the stage wall out of sight, where no one could see him. "Why am I here?", he moaned in exasperation. "Why?!"

Tweedy did not realize that being behind the stage was going to be the best thing for him after all.

The next day, his owner ran a reverb pedal off Tweedy to help him out a bit, and Tweedy responded, "Thanks, I like that!" Slowly, Dave, the sound guy, pulled up the volume on the sound board fader to bring up little Tweedy's tube sound into the sanctuary. And

through the microphone to Tweedy's heart — the tiny six inch speaker — combined with the sounds of the Telecaster electric guitar, the big hall was filled with beautiful music!

Tweedy had never heard himself like this before; he only remembered the tiny volume of his small speaker, always teased in obscurity, never thinking that one day, his tone would fill a big sanctuary from the little power tubes and the heart of his components!

Little Tweedy had passed the test of his life and all from behind a stage wall!

No longer forgotten, he had proved himself with the help of his microphone friend, his owner, and the sound guy.

"That's one of the best amps I've ever heard,"

Dave the sound guy said . . .

"Do you want to sell him?" His owner smiled and said, "No, he's not for sale. I think I'll keep him!"

Little Tweedy smiled to himself and said to his owner, "I'll stay with you and make great music in the big sanctuary if you'll help me do that by playing your Telecaster guitar."

From then on, Tweedy, the Little Champ amp had found his place each Sunday, at sixty-four years old, showing that even small things that seem insignificant in life have great power when someone believes in them and gives them a chance to shine!